tree craft

35 rustic wood projects
that bring the outdoors in

tree craft

35 rustic wood projects that bring the outdoors in

by Chris Lubkemann

Peg Couch, Style Editor

FOX CHAPEL
PUBLISHING

ISBN 978-1-56523-455-0

Library of Congress Cataloging-in-Publication Data

Lubkemann, Ernest C.

Tree craft / by Chris Lubkemann
    p. cm.

Includes index.

ISBN: 978-1-56523-455-0

1. Wood-carving. 2. Nature craft. 3. Trees in art. I. Title.

TT199.7.L8223 2010
731.4'62--dc22   45383105 3/11
                    2009044390

To learn more about the other great books from Fox Chapel Publishing, or to find a retailer near you, call toll-free 800-457-9112 or visit us at *www.FoxChapelPublishing.com*.

Note to Authors: We are always looking for talented authors to write new books in our area of woodworking, design, and related crafts. Please send a brief letter describing your idea to Acquisition Editor, 1970 Broad Street, East Petersburg, PA 17520.

Printed in China
First printing: March 2010

foreword

I live in an old home and have several even older trees in the backyard. While these trees provide much enjoyment, they also provide a lot of opportunities for work. Each spring, when the mid-Atlantic ground begins to thaw and my gardener's hands have been idle for the winter, I head to the yard to clear it of the twigs, sticks, and branches that these massive trees have dropped over the winter months. As I pile them atop my wheelbarrow, I find myself admiring the rustic bounty and thinking, "I really should make something with all of this wood." But what to make and how to make it are the questions that usually put an end to my creative daydreaming and pull me back to the task at hand. This book, however, provides the answers.

> As I pile the twigs, sticks, and branches atop my wheelbarrow, I find myself admiring the rustic bounty and thinking, "I really should make something with all of this wood."

The desire to make things by hand, and more specifically, to make things from found objects, is at the heart of the handmade craft movement. While many crafters were not thinking about sustainability ten years ago, today's crafter has become conscientious—and we want our homes to reflect that. Rather than purchase mass-produced items, we want to decorate our living spaces with handmade items that add beauty and reflect our personality. Wood is the perfect medium to do so.

Decorating with rustic wooden accents typically stirs up images of wilderness lodges and country cabins. And, while the objects in this book would certainly be right at home in those settings, we've chosen to showcase the projects in this book in a more eclectic fashion. You'll see polished silver, glass, and linen paired with items made from twigs, sticks, and branches to create a modern look that is both elegant and earthy.

The wood you find in your yard or out in nature can be transformed into beautiful and purposeful items in a variety of ways. As you will see in the following pages, a small twig can become a key chain, a branch can be sliced to make a set of chunky coasters, and a downed limb can become a hardworking coat rack. Many ideas are shared inside this book and many more ideas will most likely come to you on your own. No two pieces of wood are the same. Let the wood speak to you and see what creative ideas you can develop.

Working with found wood is not difficult but does require some basic skills, which are covered in this book. Most of the projects can be made with a simple hand saw and/or drill. If you don't know how to use these tools, I encourage you to get familiar with them. A power drill should be no more intimidating than a sewing machine. After a bit of practice with these basic tools, you'll be able to create every project in this book.

Many thanks to author and craftsman Chris Lubkemann for so thoroughly answering the question of "what can I make with all of this wood?" Chris has been honing his woodworking and whittling skills for a lifetime and has a tremendous talent in seeing the hidden potential in each and every piece of wood. The artful choices he makes in where to cut the wood, whether or not to remove the bark, and when to round the edges take his work from simple to spectacular and will help yours do the same.

I hope these projects will inspire you to get outdoors, pick up some sticks, and make something beautiful!

—Peg Couch, Style Editor

contents

introduction

Most of the carving and whittling projects described in my previous Fox Chapel books have been on the smallish side, rarely using branches more than 1" (25mm) in diameter. Also, the majority of the work has been done with a knife…in my own case, with a two-bladed pocketknife.

Many of the projects in this book are quite different in several respects. While there is a decent amount of cutting and trimming with a knife blade, much of the shaping here is done with other tools: a saw, hammer, chisel, drill, sander, draw knife, and possibly a few more.

This book is aimed not particularly at woodcarvers, but rather at folks in general who appreciate wood, have an active imagination, are creative, and like to work with a few basic tools. Of course, I'm hoping that quite a few woodcarvers, too, will find some of the ideas in this book interesting, not because there is a lot of actual carving involved in a given project, but simply because it involves a natural piece of wood that, with some creative tweaking, can be transformed into something that is unique and useful.

Have fun!

—Chris Lubkemann

how to use this book

This book is organized into six parts. Getting Started focuses on finding the wood you need, as well as covering some of the techniques you'll be using to create the projects in the following pages.

CHAPTER 1: DECORATING

(page 18) is all about projects to fill your home with eco-chic elegance. These beauties can show up anywhere: knothole photo frames in the hallway, branch candlestick holders on the mantelpiece, a stump planter on the front porch, a twig bead necklace around your daughter's neck.

CHAPTER 2: DINING

(page 48) is chock-full of tree craft pieces to deck out your dining experience. Dazzle your dinner guests with natural salt and pepper shakers, coasters, napkin rings, and more. Bring a touch of the outdoors into your kitchen (in a good way!) with a unique utensil tree and wooden spoon holder.

CHAPTER 3: LIVING

(page 68) is packed with utilitarian projects that are so simply beautiful you'll forget they're not just art. After looking through this chapter, you'll be inspired to create your own coat trees, lamps, and curtain rods. Soon your refrigerator will be bedecked with twig magnets and your living room will be graced with the presence of a natural wood coffee table.

CHAPTER 4: PLAYING

(page 102) features several fun projects and games that you'll be excited to make yourself. I dare you to check out the checker set and not want to make it! Who can resist the weathered playing surface and chunky checkers over a flimsy cardboard and plastic set? The other toys and games are just as much fun!

CHAPTER 5: WORKING

(page 114) is packed with projects to make your desk just a little more eco-chic. You'll never go back to a plastic business card holder after you peek at the naturally elegant model you could craft yourself. And why use a harsh metal knife to slash open your mail when you could have a letter opener made from the same stuff as the envelopes? Visit this chapter to remodel your desk with kinder, gentler, and more unique office tools.

getting started

The first thing you have to do when preparing to

make one-of-a-kind wooden items is find one-of-a-

kind chunks of wood to work with! After that, you'll

need to know the basic tools and skills required for

making the projects in this book. There are several

steps or procedures common to many of the projects.

Rather than repeat these in each step-by-step set of

instructions, we'll just make a general statement and

then let you apply it to where it fits.

wood

Most of the whittling/carving/woodworking I've done over the past 40-plus years has been largely with hardwood species, whether I've been working with a twig or branch from a tree or bush or making something from a piece of milled wood. However, many of the projects illustrated in this book aren't nearly as fussy in the kind of wood they call for. While I've used hardwoods for most of them, some could have just as easily be done with softer woods, even pine! The selection of wood for a given project will depend a lot on the nature of the project itself and what purpose it will serve. For instance, if you're going to make a large coat rack that will hang on an entryway wall, use a strong species of wood, both for the branch that will serve as the rack itself and for the backerboard to which the branch will be attached. Coasters for drinking glasses, on the other hand, can be from slices of almost any kind of wood, hard or soft.

To be totally honest, I don't even know the species of the wood I've used for some of the pieces illustrated in the following pages. Where it's important or useful to know the kind of wood used for a given project, I've specified what I used. Many times the choice of wood is going to be a matter of common sense, what is available, or what happens to challenge your own imagination and creativity.

FINDING WOOD

I'm a saver. My wife's a saver. When our children moved out we had to get more living space! Not that our house is huge, mind you. It's just that between our closets, attic, basement storage rooms, backyard workshop, storage shed, space under the deck, and built-on "apartment," we just about have enough room to keep what we've collected! My dear Sheri is the undisputed Queen of Shelves. If there's any horizontal surface more than $5/16$" wide, she can figure out a way to display or store something on it! (Perhaps I exaggerate a bit.) Of course, Sheri and I save different things. She saves material, construction paper, yarn, and all kinds of craft supplies, whether they come from after-Christmas deals,

WOOD	COMMENTS
Birch	Excellent. Among my all-time favorite woods.
Maple	Any maple is worth trying. Swamp maple is one of my favorites.
Cherry	Both domesticated and wild are quite good.
Beech	Can be a bit brittle, but if you're careful, it works fine.
Oak	I've made some nice pieces from pin oak, live oak, and water oak. Red oak is not particularly good.
Holly	A very hard, close-grained wood that produces beautiful pieces.
Citrus trees	Orange, lemon, tangerine, and grapefruit are good. Avoid the new, fast-growing shoots, which tend to be very pithy.
Cedar	One of the few evergreen trees I've used. There's a bit of sap to contend with.
Myrtle	Wax myrtle is good. The other varieties are worth trying, too.
Bottlebrush, Indian Rosewood, Viburnum	Several Florida woods that work well. One of my all-time favorite slingshot forks is viburnum—very, very strong and beautifully symmetrical!
Flowering Crabapple, Flowering Plum	Ornamental trees that have good branches.
Other fruit trees	Apple, peach, quince, guava. Good branches to work with.

store closeouts, or garage sales. Our grandkids just know that if there's something they want to make, Grandma has what it takes!

My saving consists of varied objects like old athletic shoes (good for painting, working in the mud, or wearing on a canoe trip—never mind that the last canoe trip I took was when my 39-year-old daughter was still in college, as I recall). And then there are boxes and piles and containers of wood: branches, blocks, strips, boards, drawer fronts, plywood sheets, bits of molding, stumps, logs…you probably get the idea. When I see a good piece of wood or an interesting branch or stump, I'll pick it up, because I know that *someday* it will turn into *something*! It's nothing to stop the car, make a quick U-turn, and go back to pick up some potential wood treasure along the side of the road. To find free and eco-friendly materials for your projects, the best thing to do is keep your eyes open. Branches and limbs are available in abundance to the observant woodworker. Drive around after a big storm; make friends with a professional tree-trimming service; and keep an eye on the trees in your neighborhood. Most people will allow you to have their downed limbs and trimmed branches in exchange for hauling them off their lawns! You can also salvage wood from furniture—remember that old broken baby crib? Or that bookshelf with the extra shelf you never could fit in? Just keep your eyes peeled and you'll be able to find whatever materials you need.

Naturally, one of the negatives of being a wood saver is you have to find a place to store what you've found until its potential is fulfilled. That

Windstorms have supplied me with quite a bit of raw material. In early spring, a storm took down one of the branches above my tree house. The nice pile of branches will turn into quite a few…well…whatevers. I haven't gotten that far yet!

Here's another tree that went down in the same storm. The Amish farmer in whose pasture it fell let me cut all of the branches I wanted. The only negative with this particular tree was that his six large mules got to the tree first and stripped quite a bit of the bark off some of the best branches! Fair enough, I guess. It was their pasture!

could mean dealing with the occasional objection of your spouse, something to the effect of, "Do we really have to have that monster slab of elm in the middle of our front porch? Ikey's going to trip over it, and Kati can't use the porch swing right!" No big deal…I just move the slab to the far end of the porch and stand it on end behind the porch swing, making sure it's angled enough

This pile displays some of my prize pieces of wood—huge trunk sections, weathered fenceposts, old floor joists—these are the types of rewards you get for keeping your eyes peeled!

so Ikey can't pull it over on himself! It takes some effort sometimes, but I'm sure you'll be able to find places to keep your treasures, too.

The fact that a lot of my own raw material for these projects has been collected over a period of years doesn't necessarily mean it will take you years to find or collect all the pieces you'll be using. If a particular project strikes your fancy and you want to make it, chances are often pretty good that with a bit of thinking and scouting, you can find what you're looking for. In some cases, though, it may take a while to come across a rather rare piece, say, for instance, a certain hollow log, or a 4-foot (1.2 meter)-diameter cross-cut slice of oak, maple, or elm. For these fairly rare pieces of wood, you'll have the challenge and fun of keeping your eyes open and making the awesome find that will allow you to produce that super-special one-of-a-kind project!

bark cleaning

Often tree bark accumulates a certain amount of dust, dirt, fungus, moss, or whatever. Before working with wood, it's always a good idea to wash off any substance that's on the bark. Dirt can soil the clean inner wood as you work on your project, rub off on clothes or furniture, and even dull your tools.

The green stuff you see on this weeping cherry stump and on these branches, as well as some of the dirt you may not see, definitely needs to get cleaned off. Gather your bark-cleaning supplies: water, a brush or rag, and gloves.

Scrub the bark with water and a rough rag or any kind of scrub brush.

If you're working with a branch or stump that has lots of little branches that can scrape your knuckles as you wash, I'd suggest wearing an old pair of leather gloves. Your hands will definitely be healthier and happier at the end of the wood-washing process!

sharpening

As for cutting the wood, making slices, etc., a variety of saws will work. Having been raised somewhat Robinson Crusoe-ish in the interior regions of Brazil and Peru, I tend to cut mostly with a regular cross-cut hand saw. Some of the aggressive toothed saws go through fairly thick pieces of wood quite easily. Of course, power saws work great, too. It just depends on what kind of tool you have at hand and are comfortable with.

In any case, **make sure the saw you use is sharp**. The cuts will be cleaner, faster, and less of an effort than if you work with a dull blade. Safer too, I might add! What is said about sharpness in relation to saw blades certainly applies to any other cutting tool: knives, chisels, planes, drawknives, files, and rasps.

There are all kinds of methods and devices for sharpening knives. I will share with you my own very simple sharpening system, but feel free to experiment and find what works best for you. This very simple sharpening system has worked extremely well for me for forty or so years, and I've enjoyed passing it on to others. Several years back, someone from Europe who worked with Nigerian doctors asked me to show him how to sharpen this way, so he could show his Nigerian colleagues how to re-sharpen their scalpels. I don't know if he actually followed through with what I showed him, but it's interesting to think that somewhere, in remote parts of Nigeria, some people may have benefitted.

Like any method or system, mine takes a little practice, but it does work, and I've been satisfied with it for quite a few years. The price is pretty

Sharpening tools (left to right): leather strop with stropping compound, various grits of wet-or-dry sandpaper, block for the sandpaper, and two different double-sided sharpening stones.

With the blade not quite flat, move it across the coarse side of the stone using a circular motion. Then, make a few slicing motions across the stone. Don't lift or turn the blade as it goes across the stone. Flip to the finer (yellow) side and repeat the same steps.

Using wet-or-dry sandpaper on top of a block of wood, use the same sharpening motions you used in Step 2. Be sure to turn the blade around to get both sides.

good, too—practically nothing, after a very small initial investment.

If I'm starting out with a totally dull knife (even a new blade can be dull), I usually use my two-sided sharpening stone to get the process started—first the coarser surface and then the finer. (Most sharpening stones have two surfaces.) With the blade not quite flat against the stone, I use a circular motion followed up by several slicing motions. After this part, the blade is semi-sharp, but not yet ready for carving.

Then I'll go to a series of little strips of wet-or-dry sandpaper or emery cloth—like the kind used on auto body work. The three grits that I generally use are 320, 400, and 600 (the higher the number, the finer the grit). Some of my little beat-up sheets have been around for eight or ten years and are still working! They're virtually paper-smooth, but they still serve to polish the blade's edge.

Finally, I'll end up stropping (wiping) my blade on a piece of leather, usually with a little bit of stropping compound. For many years, I just used the rough backside of an old leather belt.

If I'm starting with a blade that only needs a touch of sharpening, I'll start with the finest grit of wet-or-dry sandpaper and finish with a few strops on the leather.

Go through the grits—from coarser to finer. I usually use 320, 400, and 600.

Even if your pieces of sandpaper are virtually smooth, they'll still work to polish the edge of the blade.

Apply a little bit of stropping compound to your leather strop. With the blade flat against the strop, stroke it away from the edge a few times on each side.

boards, blocks, and branch slices

Before going any further, let me make just a few suggestions about the pieces of wood that will pop up in many of the projects in this book. In the case of what I've called "backerboards" or "base blocks," the pieces are generally scraps or cut-offs from milled lumber. My main sources for these have been a couple of wood shops—in one case a cabinet component shop and in the other the millwork section of a local lumberyard. Both places have been more than cooperative in letting me get wood from their scrap bins. The amount of outstanding and high quality wood I've been able to collect over the years is amazing! As far as wood slices go, it's just a matter of sawing slices and then sanding them. One important note: Make sure the branches you saw your slices from are well seasoned. If you slice a fresh or green branch, it's almost certainly going to split as it dries. A 90° cut will produce round slices, and an angled cut will give you oval shapes.

Cut-off ends provide great backers and bases. All they need is a little trimming and sanding.

Branch slices also make great bases. Big trunk slabs (much larger than these!) work well as bases for the larger projects.

Chapter 1

decorating

An elegant taper candle stretching up from a delicate

branch holder. A darling necklace made of twig beads.

The faces you love peering out from photograph frames

crafted from knotholes, fencepost gaps, and hollow

log slices. This chapter showcases projects that will

add an elegant decorative touch to your home—from

centerpieces to bud vases.

This showy hydrangea is a perfect choice for a one-stem bud vase. Try placing it by your bedside table where it won't take up a lot of room, but will add color and a pleasant aromatic scent.

bud vase

Bud vases are simply pieces of wood with a hole drilled deep enough to hold the plastic or glass tube insert that will be used to hold water and flower stems. To that end, you will need a piece of wood that will hold the tube if you want to insert live flowers. You have a lot more leeway with dried or artificial flowers, but make sure to leave enough space for the stems.

MATERIALS + TOOLS

- Piece of wood for vase body
- Piece of wood for vase base if needed
- Knife
- Sandpaper
- Glue or screws
- Glass or plastic tube
- Handheld power drill
- Drill bit to fit tube

1 Select the piece of wood that you will transform into a vase. There are shapes of naturally occurring branch formations that can be used as bud vases. I like to use simple straight pieces.

2 Flatten the bottom of the wood to give it stability. Use your saw to do the flattening work, and then finish leveling the bottom on sandpaper.

3 Drill the hole for the insert.

4 If the flattened base of the piece is wide enough, you won't have to add anything else to stabilize it. However, if you're making the vase from a thinner branch, you definitely want to add a block of wood to form a base. Find a suitable piece of wood for the base, if needed, and cut or sand it until it will sit on a flat surface. Glue or nail the base to the stem of the vase, being careful not to nail into the center of the stem because that is where the tube is going to go.

Variation

This variation of the bud vase is sturdy enough to balance taller stems. In the winter months, create a festive holiday display by inserting holly and berry stems or dried flowers.

Variation

For a fuller look, try drilling several holes into your wood. Insert a flower into each and you have an instant floral arrangement. You can create a beautiful centerpiece for any season.

BONUS PROJECT

oil lamp

Purchase a small oil lamp insert to transform your bud vase into an oil lamp. To assemble your own oil lamp innards, find a glass tube, a wick, and something to hold the wick at the top of the tube—a small porcelain drawer knob with a screw hole through it might do the trick.

MATERIALS + TOOLS

- See list for bud vase, page 21
- Oil lamp insert

BONUS PROJECT

toothpick holder

Yet another twist on the bud vase is the very useful toothpick holder. Simply make the body of the holder shorter than you would for a vase. You can attach a base or let the branch piece stand on its own.

MATERIALS + TOOLS

- See list for bud vase, page 21
- Toothpicks

Unlike small votive candles, tapers stand tall and shed lots of light. Turn off the lights and use this tall holder to create ambiance at a dinner party or other special occasion. Be sure to use no-drip taper candles.

candlestick holders

Candlestick holders are very similar to bud vases, in that they both have a well designed to hold something vertically. The depth of a candleholder hole will be between ½" and 1" (13mm and 25mm) diameter to fit the candle of your choice.

MATERIALS + TOOLS

- Piece of wood for holder body
- Piece of wood for base, if desired
- Handsaw
- Knife
- Sandpaper
- Drill bit to fit candle diameter
- Handheld power drill
- Work table

1 Select the piece of wood you want to turn into a candleholder. There is limitless variety in the shapes of naturally occurring branch formations that can be used for candle holders. Besides those seen here, you can use simple straight pieces, 2x4s, or anything else you can find!

2 If you're making your candleholder from a horizontal round log, flatten the bottom to give it stability. Use your knife to do most of the flattening work, and then finish with sandpaper. If the flattened base of the piece is wide enough, you won't have to add anything else to stabilize it. However, if using a thinner piece, you definitely want to add a base at this point.

3 Decide how many candles you want in your candleholder and use an appropriately sized drill bit to bore the holes where you want them. Use a piece of old belt as a leather protector to prevent marring of the wood.

Variation

This dual candle holder was crafted from a piece of split fire wood. It will add texture and interest to any room.

Variation

A piece of horizontal branch with the bark left on can be perfect for a candleholder—especially if you can place the candle hole just so.

Variation

No two candleholders made from branches are alike. Play up the differences by creating a mix-and-match collection. The tree bark and same colored candle will unify the elements for a cohesive look.

This versatile centerpiece can be a show stopper all year round. Surround the candle with natural touches appropriate for each season. Try miniature pumpkins, colored leaves, and small gourds in the fall and poinsettia blooms in the winter.

centerpiece ring

This ring is simply an uneven slice of the hollow log from which
I made a number of picture frames (see page 36) and a couple of
planters (see page 40). Insert whatever you want into the center
of the ring to complete your centerpiece. A pillar candle, perhaps?
Some pinecones and holly leaves? Fresh-cut wildflowers? Squash and
mini pumpkins? This project looks good decorated for any season.

MATERIALS + TOOLS

- Hollow log
- Workbench
- Materials to clean log
- Saw
- Chisel
- Sandpaper

1 Find a hollow log. This may not be the easiest task in the world, but if you keep your eyes open where there are woods, chopped-down trees, and firewood piles, there's a chance you'll run across one. When you make your find, you'll feel like you discovered a real gem!

2 Clean both the outside surface and the inside of the stump, using water, brushes, chisels, knives—whatever it takes to get the stump as clean as possible and free of any deteriorated bark or wood.

3 Using either a table or a bench as a cutting surface, saw the end of the log off flat so you have two nice clean surfaces on the finished product. Then make a second cut at an angle to form the shape of the centerpiece.

4 Once you have the ring sliced, scrape out any loose wood—I used the side of my chisel. Finally, run a bit of sandpaper around the rough edges.

Kids love to craft.
Let them help
by stringing up
this natural
wooden necklace.

necklace

Twigs and branches exist in all kinds of sizes, colors, bark textures, and grain patterns. By cutting various-sized slices from different species of wood, or even from different-sized wood of the same species, you can make a good variety of natural wood beads. By stringing them together, you can come up with a very attractive and unique necklace.

MATERIALS + TOOLS

- Assorted twigs and small branches
- Handsaw
- Workbench
- Sandpaper or belt sander
- Handheld power drill
- Bit to fit string of choice
- Finish of choice
- String

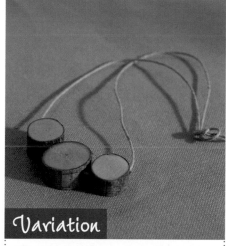

Variation

There is an endless variety of branch bead necklaces to create. Try this minimalist design.

1 Cut a whole bunch of little slices from a number of different-sized twigs and little branches. For this cutting, I especially like my little Japanese backcutting saw. Its super-thin blade makes beautiful cuts on these little branches.

2 One way or another, sand both flat surfaces of the wooden beads.

3 Drill a small hole in the middle of each piece. Try drilling some through the center of the ring (the bark will show when it's threaded), and in others drill through the ring from edge to edge (the wood grain will show when threaded). You might want to use a vise to keep the bead steady. Finish as desired and string your necklace.

Pendants are easily personalized and make great gifts. Let your kids hand them out as favors at the next birthday party.

pendant

Creating a child's pendant with a surface for personalizing is pretty similar to making a wooden bead from the previous necklace project, except that you use a single, longer piece of branch. Use a woodburner to burn on the recipient's name, or leave blank for that "modern look." It's especially fun to do the name of a person who can just never find it on one of those name racks of cups, license plates, key chains, or whatever. Even folks with fairly common names sometimes have very unusual spellings. Megan, Meagan, Meghan, Meaghan, Meaghann, and, yes, even Magin! I've even done quite a few pendants in other languages: Chinese, Japanese, Hebrew, Bengali, Hindi, Arabic, Greek, Thai, Russian, and more. Not that I know those languages. I'm just a fairly good tracer and copier. Of course, if the original I'm working from is misspelled or sloppily written, my version will be, too!

MATERIALS + TOOLS

- Assorted twigs and small branches
- Handsaw
- Workbench
- Pocketknife
- Sandpaper
- Handheld power drill
- Bit to fit string of choice
- Countersink bit
- Woodburner (optional)
- String

1 Using a saw, cut a piece of small branch about 3" (76mm) long (or longer if the person's name is a lengthy one).

2 Next, get out your whittlin' knife! Slice a swatch of bark off to create the blank spot for the name. Whittle the ends of the pendant to round them.

3 Sand the newly exposed swatch to make it nice and smooth.

4 Drill a hole through the end of the pendant for the string.

5 Use a countersink bit to clean and taper the holes a bit.

6 When you're done, you'll have a pendant with a nice clean surface ready to personalize (or leave blank). Sand out the holes if necessary.

7 Get out your woodburner and personalize that pendant!

BONUS PROJECT

key chain

Transform a pendant into a key chain by drilling the hole a little wider and inserting a key ring or loose-leaf notepaper ring. I like the loose-leaf ring because it's easy to insert and holds pretty well. For an alternate look, try leaving all of the bark on the key chain and just whittling the ends.

MATERIALS + TOOLS

- Key ring or loose-leaf notepaper ring
- See list on page 33

Milled wood can also be used to make nice key chains.

Wood photo frames seem to pop naturally out of knotholes. Fencepost holes and hollow logs also work well. You can also use these without photographs. Simply hang them on the wall as art.

photo frames

The various frames that follow in this section can be used in various ways: for photos, paintings, drawings, settings for carvings, etc. How each one is used will depend on you, your decor, and your tastes. Of course, if we're talking about a family's opinions (in other words, "you" plural), there will probably have to be some committee work and some arriving at a consensus as to how these frames are used. Regardless of their intended uses, these handsome frames will put a unique twist on your next few framing projects. Choose from hollow log slices, fencepost holes, or knotholes (or use your own imagination!).

HOLLOW LOG FRAMES

Creating a hollow log frame is very similar to making the centerpiece project on page 28. Be sure to flip to that project for further guidance.

MATERIALS + TOOLS

- Hollow log
- Workbench
- Materials to clean log
- Saw
- Chisel
- Sandpaper

1 Find a hollow log and drag it to your shop. Clean both the outside surface and the inside of the log to remove any loose bark and dirt.

2 Using either a table or a bench as a cutting surface, saw 1" (25mm)-thick slices off the log.

3 Once you have the frame sliced, scrape out any loose wood on the inside of the ring (I used the side of my chisel). Sand around the rough edges.

Hollow log photo frames are really useful for larger photos or paintings.

KNOTHOLE FRAMES

Knotholes serve as unique frames for photos, prints, or small paintings.

MATERIALS + TOOLS

- Board with knothole
- Handsaw
- Sandpaper
- Photograph or art of choice

1 Trim the board with the knothole to desired size. Smooth the edges and face with sandpaper.

2 Sand the corners to eliminate sharp outside edges.

3 Knock down any rough edges in the knothole itself. Finish as desired.

4 Next, gather the materials you want to frame (I've used photos of my grandchildren). Trim them (the photos, not the grandkids!) to fit just behind the holes, and then use masking tape to attach the photos to the back of the frames. You can also cut some thin plastic to size and make a sandwich with the photo between two pieces of plastic—this will protect the photo a bit more. Nice looking kids, aren't they? They take after their paternal grandmother.

FINDING KNOTHOLES

The best places to find boards with knotholes are woodworking shops that use milled lumber. Boards with open knotholes usually can't be used for cabinet doors or drawer fronts. Wood shops dispose of them in one way or another… firewood, wood chips for livestock bedding, and who knows what else. There's a chance that if you go to a local wood shop you'll find a board or two, or maybe even a lot more, in a scrap bin someone will let you look through. Over the past dozen or so years, I've gotten hundreds and hundreds of knothole pieces at a nearby woodworking shop. With permission from the management, a couple of the chop saw operators save the board cut-offs with open knotholes. Every so often I'll stop by and collect the little pile of knothole blocks they've accumulated under their workbench.

FENCEPOST HOLE FRAMES

Fencepost holes make unique rectangular photo frames. The old fenceposts
I used in this project are locust.

MATERIALS + TOOLS

- Fencepost
- Saw
- Sandpaper

Even without photos or art, these frames can make striking displays.

1 The first step is to find an old
fencepost with the holes in it.
Finding one will possibly be a challenge,
but when you do find one that somebody
will let you have (or maybe buy), you'll
have a unique treasure.

2 Cut the fencepost into pieces to serve
as individual frames. Sand if needed.

This planter would look just as good on the front stoop as it does indoors.

planter

This planter is a wider cut-off from the same hollow log that became a bunch of picture frames and centerpieces (see pages 36 and 28).

(see pages 36 and 28)

MATERIALS + TOOLS

- Hollow log
- Cleaning materials
- Saw
- Bench or other work surface
- Sandpaper

1 Find a hollow log. Decide how tall you want the planter to be, and then saw it off. I like to put the log on a sturdy bench and use my leg to clamp as I saw. Do what feels comfortable and safe to you.

2 Voilà! You've got a planter. Sand the edges if you want, and knock off any sharp bits inside. Find an insert that fits and put a plant in there!

Variation

Instead of putting a plant in your planter, leave the insert empty and place it next to your desk to serve as a trashcan.

stump planter

A number of years back, when we finally had our dead American elms taken down, we were left with two gigantic tree stumps in our little front yard. Our budget being kind of tight and constrained, we didn't go for the added cost of getting the stumps ground out. We had already laid out thousands of dollars to have the two enormous trees—one had grown to a branch span of 40 yards (37 meters) and the other 35 (32 meters)—taken down! What we envisioned was trying to make the stumps actually work for us. Well, our goal has been at least partially achieved. Granted, it has taken a bit of time (years), some drilling and chopping, lots of contribution from the weather, and I'm sure some grubbing around by more than a few bugs, but now we've got hollows in each stump and some fertile soil to plant in. Just add flowers!

Here's the stump in late spring of 2009.

Here is the stump a few of weeks later. Very nice, don't you think?

These two elms trees used to dominate my front yard—they reached 35 and 40 yard spans.

Wood comes in such interesting shapes and sizes. This sculptural piece conveys images of a piece of coral. It's a great conversation piece and lovely work of art for your coffee table.

table art

Occasionally, I'll stumble across a chunk of found wood that just screams to be plunked down in the middle of a coffee table and called modern art. In your searches for nifty pieces of wood, you might find something that is just plain cool all by itself. In that case, I recommend cleaning it up and letting it speak for itself!

MATERIALS + TOOLS

- Interesting piece of wood
- Handsaw
- Sandpaper
- Finish

1 Find an interesting piece of wood. A good place to look, if you want to find a piece of wood like the one shown in this project, is anywhere large bushes are being removed. The core area of a bush where the branches diverge will look like this piece of yew.

2 Clean up the wood using water and a scrub brush until all dirt is removed.

3 Cut the branches until you've shaped the tangle of branches in a way that is pleasing to you.

4 Sand the sawn faces of the branches.

5 Finish as desired.

There's so much you can do with a bare branch. In addition to using it as a Thanksgiving Tree (as shown in this photo), you can use it to decorate all year long. Spray paint it white and attach small lights for a striking holiday display.

thanksgiving tree

While I'm calling this particular project a Thanksgiving tree because of the way my family and I are using it, I'm sure it can be used in a number of other ways and for quite a few different occasions. Get it out for birthdays, wedding and baby showers, anniversaries—in short, any occasion for which you'd want to give folks the opportunity to write some little comment on a card that honors, celebrates, or thanks someone special. Another idea is to use this project as a rustic Christmas tree—string your own garland with cranberries and popcorn for an old-timey touch.

MATERIALS + TOOLS

- Branch to use as little tree
- Small log to use for base
- Handsaw
- Workbench
- Handheld power drill
- Bit to fit diameter of tree stem
- Finish
- Small clothespins
- Cards to write on

1 Find a branch or bush that has a good main stem and then forks out in all kinds of directions. Essentially, you're looking for the skeleton of a miniature tree. Strip it of its leaves. Then trim away any broken branches or ones that crowd too much. Do any trimming necessary on the stem.

2 From a decent-sized branch or small log, saw yourself a thick slice that can serve as a base for the little tree. Make sure it's wide enough to keep its balance when the mini tree is inserted. Drill a hole to fit the diameter of the tree's stem.

3 Insert the tree into the stump. If necessary, use small pieces of wood to shim the tree up straight. If you want, you can spray the whole tree with some kind of finish, or even paint.

dining

A rugged yet striking set of coasters made from firewood. A chunky log slab storing your wooden spoons vertically on your kitchen counter. An earthy napkin ring fashioned from a slice of barked branch. This chapter's collection will bring a touch of the outside into your kitchen and dining room.

Don't prevent damage to your coffee tables with just any coaster—do it in style. These wooden versions are easy to make and are sure to be a crowd pleaser. Stack them in any room where beverages might be served.

coasters

The basic idea of a coaster, as I understand it, is to provide a flat, stable surface for a glass, cup, or mug that will protect the table surface from heat or liquid damage (or both). The coasters illustrated here are extremely simple to make and will fulfill their intended purposes. At the same time, they're a bit out of the ordinary—they're original pieces of useful decoration. Different species of wood will produce a broad variety of cross-grain patterns and colors. These will especially stand out when the sliced pieces of wood are well sanded. Wait 'til you see what comes from some of the oaks!

ROUND BRANCH COASTERS

A logical source of wood for coasters is a medium-thick branch. Note: This process is what you'll do to make the checkers for your checker sets (see page 104).

MATERIALS + TOOLS

- Branch, 3"-4" (76-102mm) thick
- Handsaw
- Worktable
- Sandpaper or electric belt sander
- Finish of choice

1 Select a seasoned branch that is 3" to 4" (76mm to 102mm) in diameter. Make sure the bark is clean and tight. (See instructions on washing wood on page 14.)

2 Cut "bread slices" about ½" (13mm) thick. You can use a handsaw, with your knee on a table as the holding vise. Or, if you have an old vise worktable like mine, the cutting might be a bit easier. Regardless, when you get close to the end of each slice, slow down so you don't splinter the wood.

3 Sand the flat surfaces, either by hand on a piece of sanding belt laid on a table, or using an electric belt sander. (By the way, you can probably go to a wood shop and get an old sanding belt for nothing. While it's no longer any good for the industrial sanding machine, you'll be able to get lots of use out of it.) All you have to do now is put some kind of finish on the coasters.

Round branch slices make great coasters!

FIREWOOD COASTERS

Surprisingly, firewood makes for a sophisticated, chunky, colorful set of coasters. And the material is easy to find, too! You can use split firewood or the smaller round pieces.

MATERIALS + TOOLS

- Firewood
- Chisel
- Pliers
- Handsaw
- Sanding block
- Finish of choice

1 Start out with a nice solid piece of split oak firewood. Clean it well, removing any loose bark. Remove any long splinters. This process might involve a chisel, a pair of pliers, and a sanding block.

2 Cut ½" (13mm) slices.

3 Sand the flat surfaces of the slices as well as rounding off any sharp edges. Apply some kind of finish.

Saw some firewood coasters for your living room.

COASTER VARIATION GALLERY

Variation

A great variety of coasters can be made from round branches.

Variation

These coasters are made from a neat piece of driftwood I found.

Variation

Some clear varnish on the sides of a smooth-barked branch coaster adds a nice touch.

Variation

You can stain your coasters if you like.

Bring the freshness of the outdoors into your kitchen with this utensil tree. Try using brown or silver hooks for a refined look that matches your silverware.

kitchen utensil tree

If you have a ton of hanging kitchen utensils that you've been dying to get organized into one place, this project is for you! Depending on the size of your utensil tree, there will be room for things like measuring cups and spoons, spatulas, ladles, whisks, and whatever else you'd like to hang on the finished holder. Just one final point...boy, do tastes in interior decorating ever differ! Sort of like taste in ties, or clothes in general. What appeals to some will definitely not appeal to others. So, make something you like, appreciate, and will enjoy using. But if, when you're all done with your project, you're not really sure it's your cup of tea, there's still a good chance that someone else will absolutely love it!

MATERIALS + TOOLS

- Branch with many offshoots
- Wood for base
- Pocketknife
- Handheld power drill
- Drill bit for pilot holes
- Screws
- Brass hooks
- Finish of choice

1 Select a branch that spokes out fairly widely and in several different directions.

2 Trim off all of the little knots and branches you don't want, leaving those you do to serve as hook branches. Whittle the ends of the branches or slice them straight off—whatever looks better to you.

3 Screw the branch onto an appropriate base. Be sure to drill pilot holes and countersink the hole so you don't scratch your countertop with a screw.

4 Screw in brass hooks along the branches to hold the various utensils. Always pre-drill holes before inserting the hooks. Doing this will keep the branches from splitting. The positioning and spacing of the hooks will vary according to what utensils you want to hang where. The configuration of the branch itself will determine a lot of the hook placement. Finish as desired.

BONUS PROJECT

whisk

While you're poking around for an appropriate branch to turn into a kitchen utensil tree, you might stumble across a stick with lots of offshoots that is too small. Don't pass it by! You've just found yourself a new whisk. Peel the bark off the whisk end and partway up the handle, and you're in business!

Create these customizable name logs for your next dinner party. Let your guests take them home as reminders of a great evening.

name logs

By this time, you've realized that the projects in this chapter are the perfect accents to round out an eco-chic dinner party. If you haven't, here's your cue! These name logs are perfect for use as personalized seating labels. I made a set for my three children, their spouses, and their children. Each little log has a name and drawings appropriate to the person named. Mine has a little rooster and a whittling knife, one of my granddaughter's has a crown because she's into princesses right now—you get the idea. When I first started making what I call "name logs" quite a few years ago, my wife (who is by far more often right than wrong in her analysis and evaluation of things) said, "Who is going to buy a little stick with their name on it?!" Now, thousands and thousands of name logs later…oh well, it's a little bit affirming to be on the winning side once in a great while!

MATERIALS + TOOLS

- Pocketknife
- Sandpaper
- Woodburner
- Permanent markers

WOODBURNING

For all of the writing and drawing I do with a woodburner, I use the writing tip. It's essentially a bent wire. Some writing tips have a little ball on the end of the bent wire. In any case, make sure you use a burning tip that will allow you to write and draw easily. The sharp tips used for cutting thin lines definitely won't work for general writing and drawing. Permanent markers do a nice job for coloring simple artwork…the only kind of drawing I know how to do!

1 Remember the skills you learned for creating a pendant or key chain (see page 32)? Start with a raw, unfinished branch. Wash the bark, if necessary. Cut the branch into the lengths you want. With your knife, round the ends of the log.

2 Carefully cut out and sand the swatch on which you will be writing. **Important Note:** In spite of what you may have been told all your life, namely, "Never cut toward yourself!" there is probably not even one woodcarver on Earth who won't find that some cuts have to be made toward the body. Be careful, keeping in mind where your thumbs and fingers are and making the cutting strokes so they don't ever reach said thumbs and fingers! Wear a protective carving glove if desired.

3 Flatten the bottom of the log to keep it from rolling (if it's standing by itself) or to provide a flat surface for gluing it to a little base block or strip.

4 If you want a separate base, cut a piece of milled wood to the desired length. Sand the piece. Glue the log to the base block. Now the whole piece is ready for whatever writing and drawing you'll be doing with your woodburner and markers.

You don't have to wait for a special occasion to break out napkin rings. These rustic examples are great for everyday use. Use them with cloth napkins to cut down on paper waste.

napkin rings

Stick a nice cloth napkin into one of these rings to bring an extra touch of class to the dinner table. These sleek napkin rings will turn your next meal into a memorable event, whatever the dish!

BRANCH SLICE NAPKIN RINGS

The first type of ring is made from slices of a well-seasoned branch. (Slices from a green or fresh branch will have a tendency to split and break as they dry and contract.) There's really no rule on how thick to make the slices, but I'd aim at something close to ¾" (19mm).

MATERIALS + TOOLS

- Seasoned branch
- Handsaw
- Handheld power drill
- Forstner bit to fit desired napkin hole size
- Pocketknife
- Sandpaper
- Sanding dowel
- Finish of choice

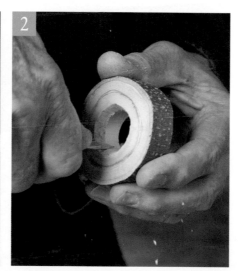

1 Slice a seasoned branch into ¾" (19mm)-thick pieces. Drill a hole in the center of the slice, holding it securely in a clamp or vise. (Don't forget the leather bark protector, a.k.a., an old belt!) For my drilling, I find the Forstner bit to be better than the paddle type bit.

2 With a knife, round the inside edges of the ring.

3 Sand the inside of the ring. I like to use a trimmed dowel or stick with sandpaper for this. Also, sand the flat surfaces and the edges of the outside of the ring. Put on some kind of clear finish.

Branch slices make for simple natural-looking napkin rings.

KNOTHOLE NAPKIN RINGS

These napkin rings are made up of a number of little square boards with knotholes. These blocks are of various species of wood. They've been trimmed and sanded around the edges, and I've tried to make sure that, even with the irregular pattern of the various knotholes, there are no sharp points that might tear a napkin. This process is essentially the same as that for making the photo frames on page 36. The only difference is that the frames are considerably larger.

MATERIALS + TOOLS

- Boards with knotholes
- Miter box and handsaw
- Sandpaper or belt sander
- Finish of choice

1 First, find some boards with open knotholes in them. You're looking for knotholes at least 1½" (38mm) in diameter. The size of the board doesn't matter—you'll be trimming that down.

2 Get out your miter box and cut around the knothole. I prefer to create square or rectangular napkin "rings" with the knothole in the middle—they are easier to saw than ovals or circles. However, if you have a band saw, feel free to experiment!

3 Now the sanding begins. Using a strip of sandpaper or a belt sander, smooth all of the flat surfaces of the ring.

4 Round the sharp edges. I like to put a facet here so the edge becomes a new face.

5 Repeat Step 4 on the corners so they aren't sharp. Apply a clear finish, and you're done!

Knotholes provide
unique napkin rings.

Interesting salt and pepper shakers like these made from tree branches are a great way to infuse creativity and personality to your table. They're also great for your picnic basket.

salt and pepper shakers

There is something very elegant, yet earthy, about using a pair of beautifully smooth-barked branches as salt and pepper shakers. The regal look of the silvery birch can be brought inside in this small way. Another way to go is to use a branch with a slightly rougher bark for a more rustic look. And don't be afraid to try some branch pieces that aren't quite straight—a fun effect results when the shakers are slightly twisted. Branch pieces with a small side twig also heighten the rustic look of the shakers.

MATERIALS + TOOLS

- Seasoned branches
- Cork
- Vise or clamp
- Leather belt
- Handheld power drill
- Forstner or paddle bit to fit desired well size
- Small twist bit
- Pocketknife
- Sandpaper
- Awl or other tool to mark shaker holes
- Finish of choice

1 Cut seasoned branches into desired lengths for your salt and pepper shakers.

2 Securing the branch in some sort of vise or clamp (notice the leather strip that is protecting the bark), drill from the bottom of the shaker, using a Forstner bit or a paddle bit that is almost the diameter of the branch. Stop the hole at least ¼" (6mm) from the end of the branch.

3 Round off the top of the shaker with a knife.

4 With a sanding block, finish smoothing the top… unless, of course, you want to have the more rustic effect that the knife cuts provide.

5 Mark the position of the holes in the tops of your shakers. Usually the salt shaker will have one or two more holes than the pepper shaker. It's your call as to the pattern and number of holes!

6 Drill small-diameter holes from the top. For the outside holes, those farthest from the center, you may want to angle them toward the center a bit to make sure they intersect with the large hole coming up from the bottom of the shaker.

7 Widen the base of the bottom hole a bit to allow for getting the cork in and out. There should be just a little space around the base of the inserted cork to allow for easy removal without resorting to a corkscrew. Apply finish of choice to the top and bottom. Be sure to treat the inside of the shaker with a food safe impermeable finish. You don't want sawdust mixed in with your salt!

8 Hardware stores usually carry an assortment of cork sizes. You'll probably have to trim a little from the length of the cork, but you shouldn't have too much trouble finding one that fits well.

Selecting branches with slightly rough bark, or segments that have a small bend in them, lend a playful personality to the resulting shakers.

BONUS PROJECT

shaker carrying tray

Try this easy-to-make accessory for your shakers. A little salt and pepper carrying tray, with little rails around the sides and a carrying stem in the middle, definitely pulls the shakers into a cohesive set.

1 Make your shakers. You'll need to know how big they are to design the tray.

2 Find a nice flat piece of wood to serve as the base. It should be big enough to fit both shakers on, as well as leave some space around the outside for the twig rails. Don't forget, you need to fit a carrying stem in the middle.

3 Cut the base to size, if needed. Sand all of the edges as desired.

4 Find a straight stick thinner than the shakers and a bit taller. Whittle one end to serve as the exposed side, and cut the other end off flat so it will sit flush against the base.

5 Drill a pilot hole through the base and handle. Countersink the hole. Screw the handle to the base.

6 Find some thin twigs to serve as the rail. Make sure you have one to fit each of the four sides of the base. Whittle the ends.

7 Finish the base and handle, as well as the twig rails, if desired.

8 I like to construct the twig rail log cabin–style, with the two ends going down first and the two long side twigs on top. Use a good wood glue to affix the twigs to each other and the base. That's it!

Adding a rustic wooden carrying tray provides yet another option for your shakers.

Put an end to kitchen clutter with these fun and functional gadget holders.

wooden spoon holder

What we're making here is essentially a small stump with a number of holes drilled in it to hold wooden spoons. Definitely no engineering degree needed!

MATERIALS + TOOLS

- Seasoned branch, at least 4" (102mm) in diameter
- Handsaw
- Handheld power drill
- Drill bit to fit size of spoon handles
- Sandpaper or belt sander
- Finish of choice

1 Start with seasoned pieces of wood. These branches will probably be between 4" and 6" (102mm and 152mm) in diameter. Cut a chunk of branch at least 4" (102mm) tall.

2 Mark the location of the holes you want to have.

3 Drill the holes, using the size drill bit that will give you the size holes you want for your spoon handles. Sand the top and bottom of the branch piece.

4 Apply finish of choice. This piece is ready for your kitchen! **Note:** Making this project with a smaller branch can yield a really neat flower vase (see page 22).

living

A beautifully simple wooden hook just where you need

one. A handsome lamp sconce crafted from a curving

tree branch. A majestic coat tree crafted from a real

tree. This chapter focuses on projects that make your

life easier and more beautiful during your time at home.

These simple projects—from a clock to an umbrella

stand—augment the beauty of your home while

remaining strikingly functional.

This unique timepiece would look right at home over a fireplace mantel. Look for wood slices with colorful heartwood and sapwood for maximum effect.

clock

You might have thought that the only way to use a tree to tell the time was to count its rings, watch its foliage progress through the seasons, or to use it as a giant sundial. Well, I'm here to tell you there's a better way! Find a slab of trunk cross-section that you like and insert some clock parts.

MATERIALS + TOOLS

- Log
- Clock parts
- Small mirror hanger
- Handsaw
- Jigsaw or scroll saw
- Sandpaper
- Finish of choice

1 Find a log that looks like you'll be able to get a good slice off of it. The log can be any diameter you think will look good.

2 Using a handsaw, saw off the slab you want. About 1" (25mm) is a good thickness to shoot for.

3 Get out your clockworks. You can recycle clockworks from an old clock purchased at a secondhand store, or you can buy new clock parts for your project. Take a look at the pieces you need. Figure out where you want the clock face to be and where that means you need to put the parts in the back.

4 Use a jigsaw, scroll saw, or whatever tool you are comfortable with to create the hole you need for the clockworks.

5 Sand the slice as desired.

6 Test fit the clockworks. Remove them.

7 Install a small mirror hanger on the back of the clock where it will be able to reach the wall and hang properly.

8 Apply finish as desired.

9 Insert the clock parts, including a battery if needed, and hang on the wall.

A rustic coat rack is the perfect way to add coat storage to your mud room or back entry way without taking up floor space.

coat rack

This rather large and heavy coat rack is intended to be well anchored to a wall. You definitely don't want to attach it to a panel of drywall with a bit of Plasti-Tac or a few strips of double-sided sticky tape! Serious screws or bolts are required, so find a stud in the wall. Once it's up, it will hold a pile of coats.

MATERIALS + TOOLS

- Hardwood branch
- Strong board
- Lag bolts
- Handsaw
- Pocketknife
- Sandpaper
- Clear finish
- Hammer
- Handheld power drill
- Twist bit to match lag bolts
- Bit to countersink holes

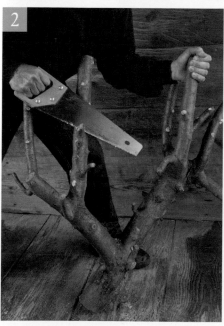

1 Choose your branch. Make sure you use a hard wood, like maple, oak, dogwood, or apple.

2 Trim off all of the little knots and branches that you don't want serving as coat pegs.

3 With your saw, trim off all the ends of the branches that remain—the ones that will be serving as pegs.

4 Round off and smooth the ends of all of the peg branches. Spray on a clear finish, if desired.

5 Now for the backerboard. Choose a good, heavy board. I think this was an old floor joist I picked up at a local secondhand store.

6 If you're using an old piece of lumber like I was, make sure you pull out all the old nails that might be sticking out.

7 Cut off a piece the size you think will be right for the particular rack branch you're using.

8 Sand off any splinters or really rough spots.

9 Position the branch on the backerboard, marking its position.

10 Drill holes in the backerboard. Make sure you have the holes angled correctly so the lag screws will go straight up the base of the branch.

11 Drill through the backerboard into the base of the branch and countersink the hole. Unless you have four arms or a pretty sophisticated clamping system, you may need someone to help you hold the branch in place while you drill the holes for inserting the screws. To be on the safe side, I'd put in at least three long and strong lag screws. As long as you're not using the wall rack for chin-ups it should be fine for holding as many coats as there are branch pegs!

Tired of coats, scarves, and backpacks slung over your furniture? Put an end to the clutter with this coat tree. It's easy to make and will add a wow factor wherever you choose to display it.

coat tree

I've made a number of standing coat and hat racks over the past several years. Some are on the narrow side and have only a few branches for hanging. Others are much wider and can accommodate a whole bunch of coats and hats. The main goal of the standing coat rack is to have a sturdy and stable piece that really serves the purpose and looks good. For a large rack of this type you'll need to look for a strong, straight sapling that branches out nicely at the top at a practical coat-hanging level. Admittedly, this particular coat and hat rack is probably way too big for my little house, but I'm sure it will eventually end up in the lobby of some restaurant or in the hallway of a much larger home where it just fits the decor.

MATERIALS + TOOLS

- Large branch or part of tree
- Slab of trunk for base
- Wedges
- Pocketknife
- Stain to match bark
- Handheld power drill
- Chisel
- Rasp
- Wood putty or other gap filler

1 The largest standing coat rack I've made so far came from a young Bradford pear tree my neighbor Tim took down because it was starting to blow over. As had happened before, Tim's loss was my gain. (One of his chopped-down maple trees provided the giant fork for my pumpkin launcher…football-field-length shots with small pumpkins!) Find a tree like this for your coat tree.

2 Trim off all the little branch tips and knots, leaving only the branches you want to serve as coat and hat pegs. Make sure all of the branch tips are smooth and rounded off. You don't want any ripped coat linings!

3 Stain and finish the whole piece. The reason I decided to stain the entire tree was to darken the spots where I had trimmed off knots and branches, making the spots blend in with the bark. Of course, some folks might prefer the reverse giraffe skin effect! It depends, I suppose, on one's decorating scheme.

4 Now for the base. For this particular coat tree, I chose a large, heavy slice of wood that had been lying outside my shop at the farm for a couple of years.

5 Working from both the top and bottom of the slice, drill and chisel out a hole in which to insert the stump of the coat rack. To get the size and shape of the hole right, make a pattern from the bottom of the stump and trace it onto the center of the base slice. This really is kind of fun…sort of like doing a giant root canal! Just try not to think bad thoughts about your dentist as you pound the chisel with your hammer!

6 Insert the stump of the coat rack into the hole in the base. With a rasp or chisel make whatever fine-tuning adjustments you need to make for a good fit. Naturally, there will probably be some gaps and spaces at various points. No problem.

7 Tap a number of long wedges into the gaps. This will tighten everything up. Check the coat rack from all sides to make sure it's straight. When you're satisfied with the final positioning of everything, cut off the wedges flush with the top surface of the base slab. Then you can use any one of a variety of fillers to close up the remaining spaces in the hole and cement the standing rack in place.

Variation

This variation on the standing coat and hat rack was a maple sapling growing in the woods in the back of another neighbor's property. (Boy, does it ever pay to have nice neighbors!) It divided itself into two convenient groupings of branches—the lower outcropping for coats and the upper one for hats. For a base, I made an X out of boards I had (see Step 4 in the Peeled coat tree on page 79) and used four small branches as braces. Everything, including the main stem of the coat rack, is secured by screws into the cross-piece base. Fitting the brace pieces took a little cutting, filing, and fine-tuning to get a good fit, but in the end the whole piece proved to be very strong and steady.

Variation: peeled coat tree

For a very different look, peel the bark off your coat tree. Also, keep in mind that you can select a smaller branch if your space isn't large enough for a tree-sized addition!

MATERIALS + TOOLS

- Large branch
- Flat lumber pieces for base
- Lag screws
- Pocketknife
- Drawknife
- Sandpaper
- Handheld power drill
- Drill bit to fit lag screws

1 For a very simple standing coat rack, let's start with the largest branch in this photo—the one on the right.

2 Using a pocketknife, strip off the bark and remove all sharp little branches and knots on the coat branches.

3 Get out your drawknife. It's been a long time since you used that, I bet! Strip the bark from the rest of the coat tree.

4 Round the coat pegs and sand the whole piece. The final step is to securely fasten the rack into a cross base. To create the cross base, get two flat pieces of lumber the same length and width. Make an X with the pieces. Attach two small blocks to the underside of the ends of the piece on the top of the X so that the ends reach the ground. Drill pilot holes through the base into the rack and insert some good, long, strong lag screws.

Strip the bark from your coat tree for a different look.

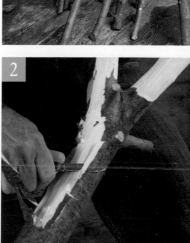

This rugged coffee table would cost a small fortune to purchase. You can make it yourself for a lot less.

coffee table

A coffee table made from a slab and a stump will really bring the outdoors into your living room. You could also build one of these rugged pieces to serve as a long-lasting, no-fuss outdoor table. Slap a couple of stumps next to it, and you've got seating!

MATERIALS + TOOLS

- Big slab of wood for tabletop
- Big stump for pedestal
- Belt sander
- Stain, if desired

1 Find a big slab of wood for the tabletop. Here's the large slice of American elm I started with. This is definitely a piece I wouldn't want to drop on any body parts!

2 Sand the top of the slab with a belt sander. I like the look of leaving the rough chainsaw cuts visible, but just smoothing out the surface.

3 I decided to stain this slab dark. Use a big stump or log as a pedestal. Use two stumps or logs if needed. You might need some shims to keep the top level. I use the weight of the slab to connect the two pieces.

4 Be sure to cover the table if you plan to leave it outside. The more you protect the wood from the elements, the longer it will last.

I really like how the tabletop looks with all the chainsaw cuts and dips.

LOG SLAB SHAPES

You never know what shapes you'll find when looking for giant slabs. Round, oval, or how about this piece? Kind of looks like the continent of Africa. I'm just about positive as to what will come out of this special slice. My older son, Steve, is a professor at George Washington University in Washington, D.C., and specializes in refugee situations in sub-Saharan Africa. And he and his family live in a great big log cabin. Wow! I can see a number of factors coming together for another great coffee table!

Who knows what shape slab your coffee table will have?

anniversary stump

When Sheri and I celebrated our 40th anniversary a couple of years ago, our children gave us a few days at a bed and breakfast in Cape May, New Jersey. Even though it was late fall/early winter, we went walking on the beach, looking at the water, the sand, the thousands of shells, gazing at the sky…and (occasionally) at each other, too! At one point on one of our walks we ran across a very eroded, water- and sand-sculpted stump that had washed up on shore. There it lay, just littering up the beautiful beach. Well, it just had to come home! A souvenir of a fun trip and a monument to another great trip that had been going on for 40 years…and the adventure continues!

1   Find your own stump or log, and an occasion to celebrate! Perhaps your son or daughter just bought their first house…why not woodburn their new address into the stump to serve as a welcome log? You get the idea.

2   Strip the bark off the stump using whatever tool feels right to you. I'd recommend a drawknife, chisel, or pocketknife.

3   Sand the wood, if needed.

4   Decorate the stump with your woodburner. You could even carve something into the stump if you wanted.

MATERIALS + TOOLS

- Log or stump
- Drawknife
- Chisel
- Pocketknife
- Sandpaper
- Woodburner

These curtain rods look best
with some sort of tabbed or
grommetted curtains that
expose the natural rod. You
can also use this rod to create
a focal point in any room
by hanging a vintage quilt,
tapestry, or rug from it. Simply
slide the rings onto the branch,
attach your display, and hang.

curtain rod

Behold—these pages will now explain how to create the cheapest curtain rod you've never purchased. I'm not sure what's the best room for a branch curtain rod. It could be a kitchen, craft room, rec room, or lanai. Completely a matter of decor and fit, I'm sure. Even if you don't have a lot of money to spend on your window treatments, these curtain rods will make your house look elegant and airy.

MATERIALS + TOOLS

- Long, straight, 1" (25mm)-thick branch
- Y branches for hooks
- Backerboards for hooks, if desired
- Pocketknife
- Screws

1 Pick a relatively straight branch that is long enough to serve the window being covered. Depending on the species of wood and the look you want, you can either de-bark the branch or leave the bark on.

2 Choose and prepare the Y-shaped branch forks that will serve as the brackets to hold the ends of the curtain rod. If desired, attach the bracket forks to little backerboards, which will in turn be screwed into the wall or window frame at the right height to hold the rod.

Form and function define
this attractive wall hook.
Make several and hang
them wherever you notice
clutter around the house.

hooks

Hooks are essentially simpler and smaller versions of the large wall-mounted hat rack we've already done. The hook branches are mounted on a backerboard fastened to a wall or door. These little guys are quite convenient to have in those places where you just need to hang something up—next to the kitchen sink for that damp dishcloth, perhaps? Or next to your bed, where you always forget to put your belt or favorite necklace someplace where you can find it in the morning? The list goes on…

MATERIALS + TOOLS

- Sturdy branch
- Milled lumber for backerboard
- Handsaw
- Pocketknife
- Sandpaper
- Handheld power drill
- Bit for pilot holes to match screws
- Screws
- Carpenter's glue

1 Choose your coat hook branches and various sized pieces of milled lumber for backerboards.

2 Trim the hook branches to the sizes you want and round all the ends of the branches. If you want to have a light-colored coat hook, remove all the bark and sand the branch smooth.

3 Cut the base of the branch according to the angle at which you want to attach the hook to its backerboard.

4 Attach the branch to the backerboard. Drill a pilot hole first, then screw in from the back of the board. For a little more strength, you might want to use a bit of carpenter's glue, too.

Use some straight branch sections and a longer backerboard to make a peg rack.

Variation

A small hook is perfect for keys or jewelry.

Variation

Mix dark hooks with light backerboards for some extra pop.

Variation

A single Y branch is yet another choice when creating hooks.

tie and belt racks

Tie and belt racks are simply slimmer versions of coat hooks. Due to their lighter loads, they don't have to be as robust. Also, they'll usually have more branches coming out of the main stem for easier storage of multiple items—as you may know, ties and belts have a way of multiplying.

MATERIALS + TOOLS

- See list on page 87

1 Find a suitable branch and backerboard.

2 Strip the bark from the branch if desired. Round the ends of the branches.

3 Spray a clear finish on the branch if desired.

4 If the branch stem is too thin to screw without splitting, drill a hole through the backerboard slightly smaller than the branch stem.

5 Using a pocketknife, whittle down the end of the branch stem until it will fit snuggly in the hole. Add glue for extra strength.

This elegant jewelry tree makes a beautiful display of all the small pieces of art that you wear every day. It would be at home on your bedroom dresser.

jewelry tree

I'll confess, I don't wear a whole lot of jewelry myself. I guess all I normally wear is my wedding ring. Oh, and my watch, if you consider that a piece of jewelry. (The very un-fancy plastic or leather band on it may immediately disqualify it, however.) My wife has some very pretty pendants, necklaces, and pins. I suppose she could hang some of her pieces on one of these trees and display them nicely, and get at them easily, too, but somehow I don't see her as the jewelry tree type. However, I'm sure there are folks out there who might appreciate one of these jewelry trees upon which to keep some of their pieces.

1 Find an interesting branch that has many natural hooks. Choose a stable base, either a log slice or a piece of milled lumber. The base itself can be made into a tray of some sort for laying out an assortment of pins, brooches, etc.

2 Prepare the branch; saw the stem off flat to match the base, cut off any extra twigs, round the ends of the twigs, and apply a finish.

3 Prepare the base by sanding and finishing as needed.

4 Drill a pilot hole (or two) from the base up through the stem of the branch. Be sure to countersink the holes so you don't scratch whatever surface you sit the jewelry tree on.

5 Screw the branch to the base. Voilà!

MATERIALS + TOOLS

- Interesting branch with many natural pegs
- Log slice or milled lumber for base
- Handsaw
- Pocketknife
- Sandpaper
- Finish
- Handheld power drill
- Bit for pilot holes
- Countersink bit
- Screws

Variation

This elegant jewelry stand has the appearance of a windswept tree.

Variation

Remember the kitchen utensil tree from page 54? Well, it turns out that you can quite easily hang jewelry from those hooks in place of measuring spoons! Use your imagination and you'll never run out of project ideas.

BONUS PROJECT

trinket tree

This trinket tree has been standing in my shop at the farm for quite some time. Many people have wanted to buy it over the years. I like this piece too much to sell it, but it's not too hard to make one of your own, provided you can locate the right branch. You can use this project for many different things—you can hang things on it, sit little bric-a-brac on the flat surfaces—whatever you want.

MATERIALS + TOOLS

- Branch with lots of thick offshoots
- See list on page 91

1 The "right" branch for this project will be thicker than one you'd use for a jewelry tree. You want the offshoots to be thick enough that, when a flat surface (parallel with the ground) is sawn on it, it is big enough to sit a little trinket on. Locate a nice thick base as well.

2 Trim off any unneeded branches.

3 Saw off the offshoots so you have lots of little flat stages to perch items on. Saw the bottom of the branch so it fits nicely on the base.

4 Sand the flat surfaces you just created.

5 Finish the branch if desired.

6 Drill a pilot hole and countersink it.

7 Attach the branch to the base.

Lamps do more than just shed light. They are an integral part of any decorating scheme. These are just a few of the possibilities. Experiment with different shades to complement your space.

lamps

The possibilities for crafting lamps from wood are almost endless. I've included instructions for table lamps and sconces here, but this is the type of project where you can really exercise your imagination and creativity. What about a floor lamp? A desk lamp? A lava lamp? Making lamps has certainly been a lot of fun for me!

MATERIALS + TOOLS

- Piece of wood for lamp body
- Block or branch slice for lamp base
- Lamp hardware
- 4 feet for lamp base
- Screws
- Work table
- Piece of old belt
- Long drill bit
- Handheld power drill

1 All of these natural stumps and branches have potential for making good lamp stems. Whatever piece you happen to be using, cut it to the length you want for your lamp. Make sure your cuts are straight so the lamp stands vertically and isn't leaning one way or another.

2 Secure the piece in some kind of clamp, work table, or vise. (I've been using this old Black and Decker Workmate since the mid-1970s, and it's still going strong!) To keep from damaging the bark when I tighten the clamp, I almost always wrap a thick piece of leather around the branch. A piece of old belt usually does the trick.

3 With a drill bit that is long enough (in this case, an electrician's bit), drill through the branch from the center of the top. Where the bit comes out at the bottom end is not really critical, as long as it does indeed come out at the bottom and not somewhere on the side of the stem.

4   Select a base block or branch slice for the base of the lamp and screw it into the stem. You'll need to glue four little feet to the bottom of the base to allow for the lamp cord to come out. Then, drill down from the top of the stem and through the base piece. Voilà, you're ready to feed the electric cord through and attach the light and shade holding fixtures!

5   Attach all of the fixture-holding hardware. You'll probably find that you need to open up a little wider well of about ¼" to ½" (6mm to 13mm) deep at the top of the lamp stem to give enough space for the lamp fixture hardware to fit into the stem. Make sure you securely screw the little plate that's holding the bulb fixture and the harp, which in turn will be holding the lamp shade.

Variation: firewood table lamp

This variation is one of my favorite recent lamps. It's made from something you might have stacked in your backyard right now—a chunk of oak firewood. Split firewood, as well as the smaller, round pieces, can provide a tremendous variety of lamp stems. Variations in shapes, knot locations, and grain patterns make for very original and beautiful pieces. (Okay, beauty is indeed in the eye of the beholder, so we'll leave the choice of what is beautiful up to you!)

FINDING LAMP HARDWARE

Let me share a little about getting the hardware parts for lamps. Of course, one can go to a store that sells wire, light sockets, plugs, nipples, washers, screws, nuts, and shades, and buy everything brand-spanking new. Or you can go the recycling route like I did, and for very little buy a bunch of old lamps from the local secondhand store. While not all of the shades were in good shape, the wires, sockets, and other parts were just fine.

1   Choose a piece of firewood and clean off any splinters (there definitely will be some!) with a chisel.

2   Sand the whole piece so that even with its semi-rough look, there are no sharp points or small splinters on which to catch a finger. From here, continue with Step 1 from the first lamp project.

sconce

Sconces are simply smaller lamps designed for hanging on a wall or the side of a cabinet. The sconce featured here usually lives on the side of a cabinet just to the right of our kitchen sink. It fits in great with the rest of the decor in Grandma Sheri's jelly-making, cookie-baking country kitchen!

MATERIALS + TOOLS

- Curved branch
- Chisel, knife, or router
- See list on page 95

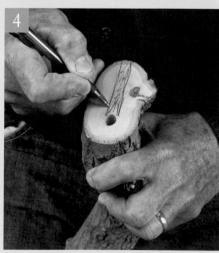

1 Select a branch that will jut out from a wall or flat backerboard. This might be a slightly curved branch or one like this one that has a distinct elbow. Cut the branch to get the angle you want on the backerboard and for the top that will hold the light fixture.

2 Drill down from the center of the light fixture end all the way through the elbow. You'll have to use a long bit to get all of the way through.

3 Drill from the backerboard end until you intersect with the hole coming down from the light fixture end. A good way to sight and aim this particular drill "shot" is to leave a long rod, dowel, or drill bit sticking out of the first hole so you can use it to line up your second hole.

4 Draw a little canal or groove that you can cut out with a chisel, drill, knife, or router. This groove will provide a recessed exit for the wire coming from the fixture through the branch and to the plug and outlet. If you want, you can make this groove in the back and bottom of the backerboard instead of in the base of the branch. Screw the fixture into the top of the sconce stem. Don't forget about the little well you'll need to fit the fixture into the wood.

Have your kids draw on these miniature
canvases so they can display their
artwork on the refrigerator all the time.

magnets

One little item that has pretty well become as institutionalized in America as apple pie is the refrigerator magnet. Granted, quite a few homes now sport stainless steel refrigerators—to which magnets don't stick—but hey, I bet they can put up a cookie sheet that'll work! Magnetic paint is also an option. What we're making here are essentially miniature plaques to which magnets can be glued and designs can be woodburned.

MATERIALS + TOOLS

- Seasoned branch
- Handsaw
- Sandpaper
- Woodburner
- Permanent markers
- Finish
- Glue
- Magnets

1 Cut thin slices from a seasoned branch. These can be cut either straight or at an angle, depending on whether you want the mini-plaques to be round or oval-shaped.

2 Sand the flat surfaces smooth.

3 Woodburn whatever designs you want. For coloring the designs, I generally use permanent markers.

4 If you want, you can spray or brush some kind of finish on the piece.

5 Glue a magnet on the back of the finished mini-plaque. I've almost always used yellow carpenter's glue, but you may want to use hot glue or some other type of adhesive. Make sure to pick the big magnets so those treasured report cards and pieces of artwork don't slide off the fridge!

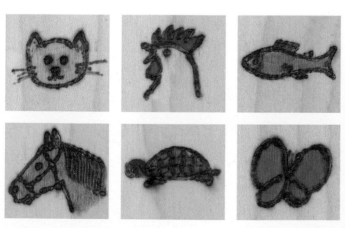

This sturdy umbrella stand works well in a setting where umbrella stands are perpetually being knocked over.

umbrella stand

All kinds of factors, including a nice discovery on your part, plus a little work, can produce a unique stand for umbrellas. This piece can find a spot either on your covered front porch or in the hallway just inside your front door.

MATERIALS + TOOLS

- Hollow stump or log
- Hammer
- Chisel
- Stiff brush
- Nail or small screwdriver
- Sandpaper
- Finish of choice

1 Start with a hollow stump. Naturally, the inside of the stump will be deteriorated. No problem, as long as there is still a good, thick rim of solid wood that will be left when all the soft and loose parts are cleaned off.

2 With a hammer and chisel, remove all of the bark. One reason you want to take the bark off is that you don't want to leave any hiding places for wood chomping critters to hang out in. With a stiff brush, go over the whole outside surface of the stump, making sure to clean out any little grooves (some of them beautifully etched by the aforementioned little critters!). You may have to use a nail or the tip of a small screwdriver to get into some of these small spaces.

3 Using a hammer and chisel, clean out all of the soft or deteriorated wood from the inside of the stump, making sure to cut out any interior knots, splinters, or other sharp points that could tear an umbrella.

4 Besides using a chisel, you may want to use a wire brush, or sandpaper wrapped around a good-sized stick (maybe even around an old baseball bat!). While the finished inside surface of the stump won't be perfectly smooth and will still have many natural (and desired) dips and waves, just make sure you're satisfied that it is indeed a good receptacle for nice umbrellas. Put some kind of stain or finish on the whole stump—your choice!

Chapter 4

playing

A sturdy checker set cut into a stump. A tightrope

walker that balances miraculously on a taut string.

A unique croquet set that your children and

grandchildren will love. This chapter focuses on

fun toys and games crafted playfully from wood—

straight from nature to your living room.

Friends and neighbors
are sure to gather in your
yard with the addition of
this oversized checker set.
Have some fun and start a
neighborhood competition.

checker set

For most of the forty-plus years that I've been carving and whittling branches, I've considered myself more or less a miniaturist. Even the pieces that I considered large have been considered small by other folks. This project has definitely taken me way out of character! This large checker table is another slice from the trunk of one of the giant American elm trees that once graced my front yard. One of these elm trees had a branch span of 40 yards (37 meters) and the other 35 (32 meters). Sadly, a number of years back they both succumbed to Dutch elm disease. From their stumps and branches, however, have come quite a few unique pieces.

MATERIALS + TOOLS

- Big slab for top
- Stump for pedestal
- Stumps for stools
- Checkers (follow directions on page 51)
- Belt sander
- Measuring tape
- Carpenter's square
- Straight edge
- Pencil or pen
- Hammer
- Chisel
- Small brush
- Dark stain
- Clear finish, if desired

1 Start with a nice thick slice of tree trunk. This particular slice came from a spot farther up the trunk where the largest branches were already beginning to branch out. I've never weighed this slice, but believe me, it is heavy! Definitely not something you want to drop on your toe!

2 Sand the top surface of the slice. For my own table, I decided not even to try to sand the surface perfectly level and smooth, but rather to let the chainsaw marks and irregularities remain to add character to the finished piece. What I did do was use the belt sander to take out any sharp edges and the harsher or really pronounced dips and drop-offs.

3 After sanding the top to a reasonably smooth surface, I measured out the 64-square grid. Naturally, the size of the grid and squares will depend on the dimensions of the slice of wood. Just make sure you draw a board that is 8 squares by 8 squares, and do your math correctly. Good practice on fractions!

4 With a hammer and chisel, I notched out the lines for a regulation checker board. I suppose I could have used an electric router and done the lines faster, but I just kept with the Robinson Crusoe technique and went the old-fashioned way. In any case, I was happy with the results.

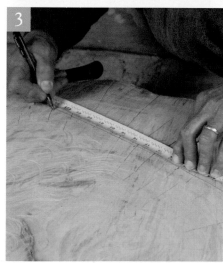

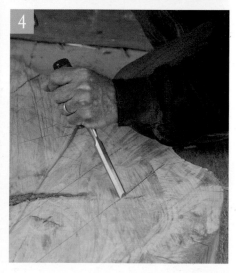

5 With a small brush, carefully stain every other square dark. On a piece of wood this size there will be a certain amount of natural checking over time, but these little splits and check marks just add character to the piece.

6 Follow the directions on page 51 to make the checkers. You'll need 12 light checkers and 12 dark checkers. Use the stain you painted the dark squares with to stain the dark checkers.

7 Use a good-sized stump for a pedestal and set the top on it. You may have to use a shim or two to make sure the top is level on the stump if the adjoining surfaces aren't even. I've never tried to connect the two pieces, just laid the top on the base. The weight factor alone keeps everything stable and steady. Even so, I wouldn't recommend tap dancing on the edge of the table top! A couple of smaller stumps can serve as stools for the players to sit on.

8 If you're planning on leaving your checker table outside, exposed to the weather, be sure you cover it. My first set has been outside my shop at the Amish Farm and House for years, has been played on by thousands of people from all over the world, and is still in great shape. Every night, and before any rain during the day, I cover it with a cloth and a couple of layers of plastic or tarp, with a weight to keep them from blowing off.

small checker stump

This checker board was created from the stump of a weeping cherry tree that my neighbor Mark cut down not too long ago. The project uses the same basic process as the large checker board, just on a smaller scale. No pedestal is needed on this one.

MATERIALS + TOOLS

- Small log or stump
- See list on page 105

1 Find a nice little chunk of log or stump, probably about a foot (305mm) across or so.

2 Sand the top surface with a belt sander. Draw in and carve the checker squares as shown for the big slab checker set. Stain every other square.

3 Use a handsaw to cut 24 checkers from a medium-sized branch. Stain half of the checkers with the same stain that you used on the board.

This small checker set can nestle in equally well next to your sofa or in the backyard.

This mini croquet set makes a great indoor activity for those rainy or wintery days. Have your kids make up their own rules.

croquet

Nothing like a game of croquet out in the summer grass! But what if you get a hankering to play the game during the winter months? This set allows you to bring the fun of the outdoor game into your living room. I've made my set smaller than a normal croquet set in addition to making a few modifications for indoor play.

1 Find some nice straight branches to turn into the mallet handles. You'll also need a thicker branch—about 2" (51mm)—for the mallet heads. I usually make four mallets, but you can have as many as you like!

2 Drill a hole partway through the mallet head for the handle. The hole should be slightly smaller than the diameter of the handle branch.

3 Whittle down the end of the mallet branch until it fits snuggly in the hole you drilled. Add some glue for extra security.

4 Next, let's work on the wickets. Get enough thin flat lumber for the bases of nine wickets. Drill two holes the diameter of a coat hanger wire, and bevel the front and back edges of each base (I use sandpaper or a belt sander) so the ball will roll easily through the wicket.

5 Use wire cutters to cut the hook off nine wire coat hangers. Bend the wires into an arch. Next, bend the end of each wire perpendicular to the wicket, and away from the other end. This way, the wire will be stable, with one foot pointing forward and one backward.

6 Thread the wire wicket into the base through the holes you drilled earlier. Tape down the wire feet underneath the base if desired.

7 Make two stakes. You'll need thin flat lumber for two bases, as well as a medium-thick straight branch to form the stakes themselves.

8 Drill a pilot hole through the base and stake. Countersink the holes. Attach the stake to the base using a screw.

9 Finally, decorate your mallets, wickets, and balls as desired. Traditionally, the balls are colored, but feel free to differentiate them with designs. One ball could be striped; one could be polka-dotted; one could have flowers on it; you get the idea.

MATERIALS + TOOLS

- Straight branches for mallet handles and stakes
- Thicker branches for mallet heads
- Flat thin lumber, enough for nine wicket bases and two stake bases
- Wooden balls of any size from craft store
- Handheld drill
- Bit to match mallet handles
- Bit to match coat hanger wire
- Bit to match screws for stakes
- Countersink bit
- Pocketknife
- Glue
- Nine wire coat hangers
- Wire cutters
- Sandpaper or belt sander
- Screws
- Woodburner

Insert the hoop through the holes and then bend one foot in one direction and the other in the opposite direction.

A tightrope walker would be a fun addition to a child's bedroom or playroom, not to mention a classroom.

tightrope walker

This little guy crossing a tightrope is really simple to make. It's just a matter of playing around with a stick man–shaped branch, making some notches, and setting him up with a long, bent pole (either a thin branch or a length of wire clothes hanger) connected to a couple of counter weights. To connect to the wire to the man you'll need to make some notches on his hands and on his chest just below his arms. Oh, and to keep him from slipping off the fish line, make sure you cut a notch on the bottom of each foot!

MATERIALS + TOOLS

- Stick man branch
- Long thin twig for balancing pole
- Chunks of branch for counterweights
- Pocketknife
- Handheld power drill
- Bit to match balancing pole
- Fishing line, floss, or some other type of line

1 The first step is to find a natural stick figure shaped like a tightrope walker—one leg in front of the other, and arms balancing outward. As you can see, they come in many sizes. Carve a face on the stick man if you want. Carve a line in his feet so he'll stay balanced on the wire.

2 Find a long, thin twig to serve as the balancing pole. Bend it a bit so it'll fit right into the stick figure's arms. Position it on the stick figure and cut notches into his arms so the twig won't slip out.

3 Next, carve down the ends of the twigs so they are sharp. Get two counterweights—chunks of branch—and drill a small hole in the end of each. Push the twig into the counterweights. Finally, put the tightrope walker on his wire and adjust the counterweights until he balances. Ta-da!

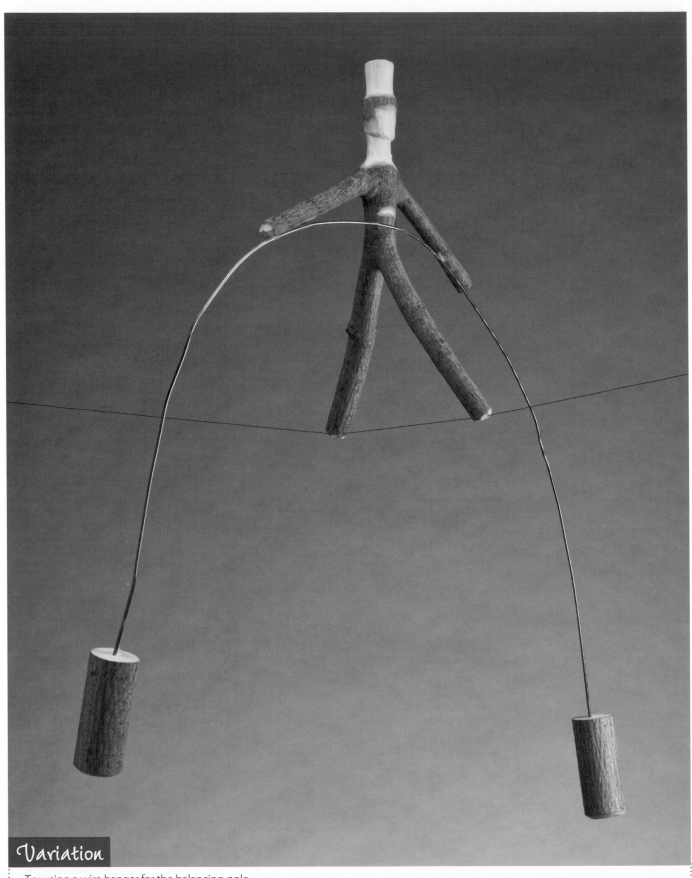

Try using a wire hanger for the balancing pole.

KNOTHOLE SHAPES

Did you ever look at clouds and try to see different things: a wolf, a trumpeting elephant, an alligator just about to swallow a duck, or maybe even a pretty good likeness of your Aunt Sally? Well, you can do some pretty interesting shape-finding with natural knots, knotholes, and grain patterns found in wood. Over more than a decade, as I have been collecting knothole cut-offs at Keystone Wood Specialties just down my street, I've run across all kinds of shapes that remind me of different things. My friend, Shelly, the woodworker who for years has been my main knothole saver, has become really adept at discovering and identifying many of these shapes. While you're making the projects in this book, you might come across some cool knotholes that jump out at you as looking like a specific thing. Why not make a game out of these knotholes? You could set it up as a matching game with specific answer cards. Or what about a "box of clouds" for that rainy day when you can't lay out on the grass and look for clouds shaped like dogs and trees and muffins…well, you get the idea.

The letter G

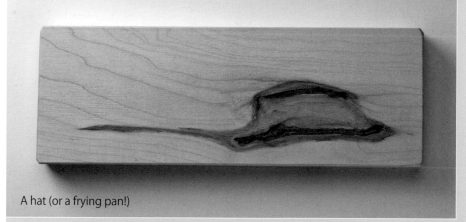

A hat (or a frying pan!)

A bull's head

A bird

A heart

working

A business card holder your clients will really notice.

A letter opener harvested from among the branches

of a tree. A distinctive desk set that's a far cry from an

old coffee mug. This chapter's projects will bring the

clean elegance of the outdoors right onto your desk.

Counter balance the hum of office electronics with this warm wooden business card holder. Make two and use one at home to display phone messages and notes to family members.

business card holder

Business card holders can be made by combining a name log, a milled wood base block, and another piece of milled molding or cut-off. Woodburning and decoration add the final touch. You can also use this project as a note holder or whatever else you can think of!

1 Find a stick for the front of the business card holder. Shave a swatch of bark off, and sand that area. Trim the ends of the stick. Cut a flat spot so the stick will sit flat on the base.

2 Find or cut a piece of milled lumber for the base. Sand the edges and the faces so they are smooth.

3 Find a short piece of molding. Sand the edges and glue or screw it to the base so it will serve as a support behind the cards.

4 Glue the stick on the front of the base to serve as a stop for the cards.

5 Woodburn as desired!

MATERIALS + TOOLS

- Stick
- Piece of molding
- Piece of milled lumber for base
- Sandpaper
- Glue
- Woodburner

Variation
Try woodburning your website, name, or whatever other information you need onto your new business card holder.

Make the chore of sorting through mail a bit more tolerable with this twig-carved letter opener. It also makes a great gift for any dad or grad.

letter opener

A letter opener is just a wooden knife intended for use opening envelopes. It can be of almost any size and be carved from either a branch or a piece of straight-grained milled wood. Before long, you'll be slitting open envelopes with style!

MATERIALS + TOOLS

- Straight branch, free of knots
- Pocketknife
- Fine grit sandpaper
- Woodburner (optional)

1 Choose a straight branch that is free of knots. If the branch has a slight curve, make sure that when you carve the blade, you end up with a blade that is straight when you look at it from the top. Seeing the curve of the branch from the side is fine. If there is any knot on the branch, it should be either at the butt end of the handle or at the spot where the handle transitions to the blade.

2 With your knife, flatten both sides of the branch to make the blade, leaving the handle portion round.

3 Finish shaping the blade, notching the division between the handle and the blade.

4 With fine grit sandpaper, smooth and sharpen the blade. Finish the opener as desired. All kinds of variations can be done with the handle, both in terms of the carving itself and in the burning and decoration.

Variation

Just look at the variety of letter openers here! It all depends on the branch and your imagination.

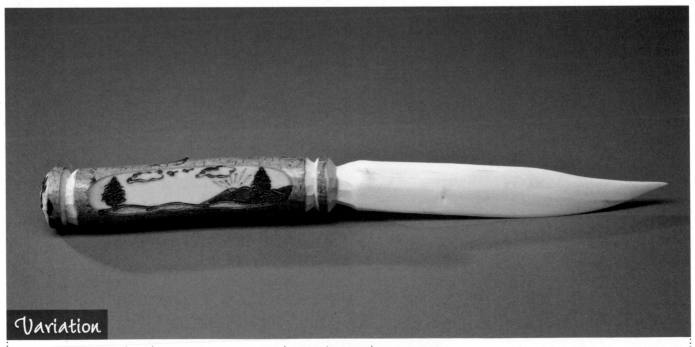

Variation

You can go very simple with your opener, or you can decorate it as much as you want.

spreader

This spreader is a spin on the letter opener project. By simply making the blade rounded and wide, you've got yourself a great kitchen tool for spreading mayonnaise, peanut butter, and who knows what else! You could further modify this project to make a serrated knife, a spatula, a spoon, a slotted spoon, a cake server…it's up to you. Just find the right branch and you can make any serving tool you like!

MATERIALS + TOOLS

- See list on page 119

1 Shape the handle of the spreader. Cut grooves in the handle if desired.

2 Move on to the blade of the spreader. Slice the branch down on both sides until you've got a thin flat blade. Sand the spreader blade so it is smooth on all sides.

Substitute this stylish pencil holder anywhere you've been using a mug to hold writing implements.

desk set

The basic idea here is to make a piece that holds pens and pencils—maybe even crayons, markers, brushes, or scissors—on a desk or table. Just about any piece of wood that can be drilled with a series of holes will do the trick. It can be a horizontal log, a vertical stump, or any other shape that can be made steady enough to hold writing or drawing utensils. For added stability, if the log or stump might roll or fall over, you can glue or screw it to some kind of broader base. The base can either be left plain, or it can be woodburned with a person or company's name.

MATERIALS + TOOLS

- Piece of branch or log
- Wood for base, if desired
- Handsaw
- Pocketknife
- Handheld power drill
- Bit to fit desired writing implements
- Sandpaper
- Finish of choice
- Glue or screws
- Woodburner (optional)

1 Choose the main piece of wood for the desk set. It could be a chunky piece of log sitting upright, with the pencils growing up like shoots; it could be a horizontal log with holes drilled along the top; or it could be something else entirely! Determine if you need a base or not, and select that if you do.

2 Prepare the main piece—trim the ends, strip the bark, whatever you think looks good.

3 Drill the holes in the main piece, using a bit that will create holes properly sized to fit whatever writing implements you plan to store in your desk set. I also find that countersinking these holes makes a nice appearance.

4 Sand any exposed wood grain on the main piece.

5 If you're using a base, cut it to the shape you want, bevel the edges, and smooth all of the faces with sandpaper.

6 Attach the base to the main piece using glue or screws. Be sure to countersink any screw holes, and keep them out of the way of any pencil holes!

7 Woodburn your name or company's name into the base if desired.

8 Finish as desired.

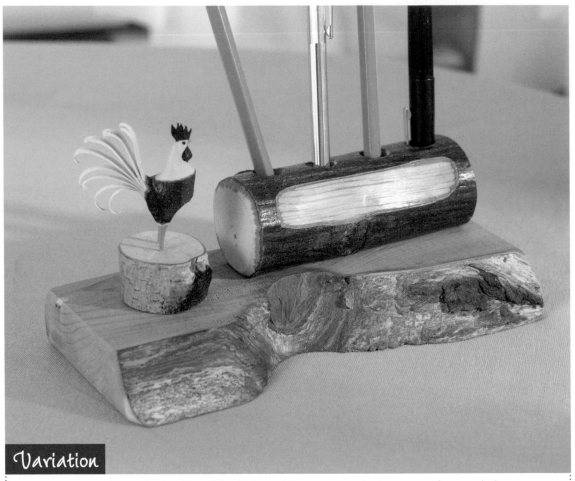

Variation

Try using a piece of natural-edged wood for the base. You can even whittle a rooster for your desk set, if you're inclined to!

Variation

These chunky stump desk sets are made from thicker branches.

Variation

A nice straight branch with some interesting knotholes makes a great kid's colored pencil holder.

dedication

This book is dedicated to my wife, Sheri, who for more than 42 years has been lovingly tolerant (for the most part) of my wood collecting, wood storing, and woodcarving. While she's not a carver herself, she is a great appreciator of wood and what can be done with it. She has been a great encourager along the way, not just in my work with wood, but in *life*.

acknowledgments

A while back, I approached Fox Chapel Publishing with a suggestion for another book of carving projects to follow up the two previous books we had done together, my target audience being basically the same folks that had responded well to *Whittling Twigs and Branches* and *The Little Book of Whittling*. What Peg Couch, Fox's acquisition editor, came back to me with was interest in another book, yes, but taking a different tack as far as content and aiming at a much broader audience. Peg asked if I could do a book that would follow an "eco-chic" theme, doing projects related to home use and decorating; in other words, recycling wood resources from the outdoors and bringing them inside in useful, creative, and fun ways.

To be totally honest, while the project did seem like something I might be able to do, I was extremely amused at the thought of me doing an "eco-chic" book. "Eco," no problem. That concept fits well with my early youth in the interior parts of Brazil and Peru: rainforests, tree-houses, dugout canoes, rafts, riverboats, alligators, snakes, spiders, piranhas, kerosene lanterns, slingshots, traps, and hours and hours spent climbing trees. Even as an adult, I've done lots of Robinson Crusoe-ish improvisation and construction. But the "chic" part! I'm quite sure anyone who knows me even half decently would get a big chuckle, if not a shoulder-heaving laugh! "Chris…chic? I don't think so!"

So here's the formula for the book, in broad terms: I'll take responsibility for the "eco" use of the raw materials and the making of the various projects that follow. Peg Couch and Kerri Landis and their gang (including Lindsay Hess, Scott Kriner, and Troy Thorne) get the lion's part of the credit for all of the chic uses and applications. Peg's home served as the main staging area for many of the final inside photos. And Troy (Fox Chapel's art director) lent his backyard as the

The goats at The Amish Farm and House definitely appreciate recycled wood! They climb on old cable spools and other scraps that have been transformed into their own personal playground.

setting for a number of outdoor shots. So, my deep thanks to the whole Fox Chapel Publishing team (those mentioned above and I'm sure many others) for all they did to take my "eco" and make it "chic"!

I'm very grateful to Sam Stoltzfus, the owner of Keystone Wood Specialties, for allowing me over the past twelve or so years to gather thousands of beautiful wood scraps of all sizes and descriptions. I've been able to sand, cut, trim, and carve these pieces into countless projects that have traveled far and wide. Special thanks to chop saw operator Shelly Bitler, who has saved hundreds and hundreds of open knothole pieces for me, and to Gabe Myers, who now works at the saw and keeps saving me those special little cut-offs. And thanks to Tim, Tom, and other Keystone workers who have contributed pieces of wood to my "this-will-turn-into-something" pile.

My special appreciation to The Amish Farm and House for letting me use the east bay of their beautiful 1803 stone bank barn as a temporary workshop and a great setting for many of the "how-to" photos in this book. And of course I'm very grateful for my little corner shop in the smaller barn just behind the farmhouse. It's where I do most of my carving Monday through Saturday, April through October. It's a great place to work. Where else can a person cut up all he wants and still stay out of trouble?! It's also just 30 seconds away from a whole herd of pygmy goats, who themselves are some of the greatest appreciators of what can be done with recycled wood!

STYLE EDITOR: Peg Couch
COPY EDITOR: Paul Hambke
DESIGNER: Lindsay Hess
EDITOR: Kerri Landis
EDITORIAL ASSISTANT: Liz Norris
INDEXER: Jay Kreider
PHOTOGRAPHER: Scott Kriner
PROOFREADER: Lynda Jo Runkle

More Great Books from Fox Chapel Publishing

The Little Book of Whittling
Passing Time on the Trail, on the Porch, and Under the Stars
By Chris Lubkemann

Unwind while you learn to create useful and whimsical objects with nothing more than a pocket knife, a twig, and a few minutes of time.

ISBN: 978-1-56523-274-7
$12.95 • 104 Pages

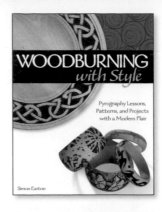

Woodburning with Style
Pyrography Lessons, Patterns, and Projects with a Modern Flair
By Simon Easton

This beautifully photographed, hands-on instructional guide to the art of pyrography will take you on a journey of skill-building exercises that begin at the basics to finish with stylish, gift-worthy projects.

ISBN: 978-1-56523-443-7
$24.95 • 160 Pages

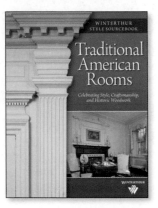

Wooden Bowls from the Scroll Saw
28 Useful and Surprisingly Easy-to-Make Projects
By Carole Rothman

You will not believe these bowls were made without a lathe! Includes 28 easy-to-make projects for crafting beautiful bowls and more with a scroll saw.

ISBN: 978-1-56523-433-8
$19.95 • 136 Pages

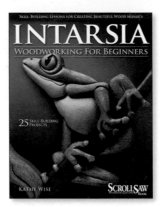

Intarsia Woodworking for Beginners
Skill-Building Lessons for Creating Beautiful Wood Mosaics
By Kathy Wise

You will learn everything you need to know to make beautiful intarsia artwork—from cutting basic shapes and sanding to stack-cutting and creating depth.

ISBN: 978-1-56523-442-0
$19.95 • 128 Pages

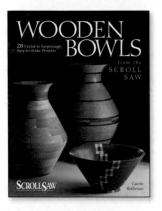

Traditional American Rooms
Celebrating Style, Craftsmanship, and Historic Woodwork
By Brent Hull

Immerse yourself in the elegance and character of historic American architecture with this guide to the magnificent millwork of the Winterthur Museum and Country Estate.

ISBN: 978-1-56523-322-5
$35.00 • 184 Pages

Homemade Halloween
Quick and Easy Costumes, Decorations, and Not-So-Frightening Family Fun
By Fox Chapel Publishing

Making your house the spookiest on the block has never been easier. You'll find fun, affordable, and creative ideas for "no sewing" costumes, stress-free party recipes, "no-carve" jack-o-lanterns and more.

ISBN: 978-1-56523-382-9
$14.95 • 84 Pages

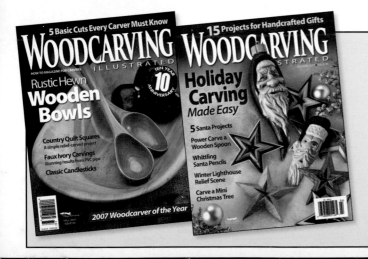

WOODCARVING
ILLUSTRATED

In addition to being a leading source of woodworking books and DVDs, Fox Chapel also publishes *Woodcarving Illustrated*. Released quarterly, it delivers premium projects, expert tips and techniques from today's finest carvers, and in-depth information about the latest tools, equipment, and materials.

Subscribe Today!
Woodcarving Illustrated: **888-506-6630**
www.FoxChapelPublishing.com

Look for These Books at Your Local Bookstore or Woodworking Retailer
To order direct, call **800-457-9112** or visit *www.FoxChapelPublishing.com*

By mail, please send check or money order + $4.00 per book for S&H to: Fox Chapel Publishing, 1970 Broad Street, East Petersburg, PA 17520